A Big, Blue Box

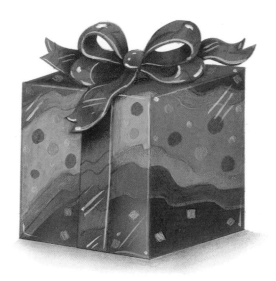

Written by Carolyn Rossetti
Illustrated by Patti Boyd

Scott Foresman

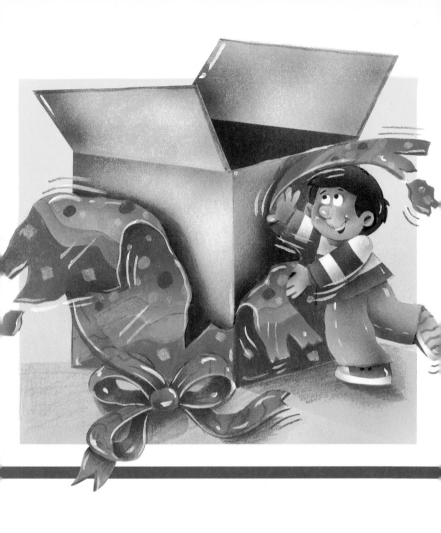

In a big, blue box,

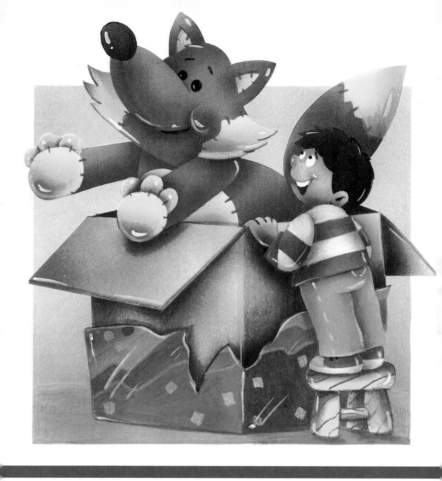

sat a big, big fox,

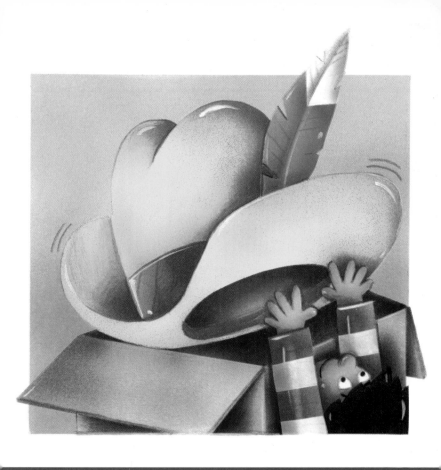

and a big, yellow hat,

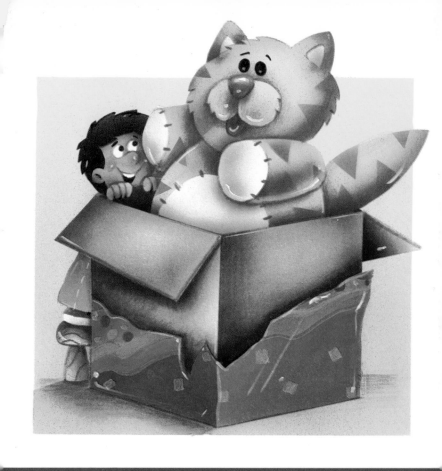

and a big, yellow cat,

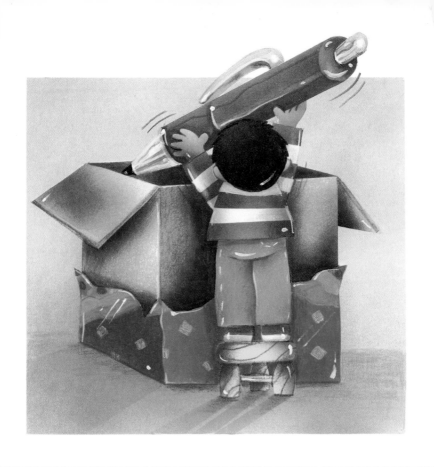

and a big, red pen,

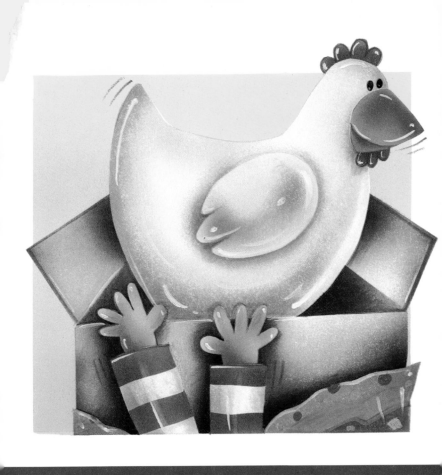

and a big, big hen,

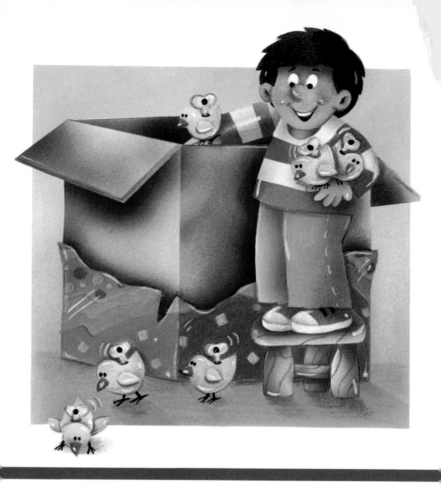

and six little, little chicks.